REMINISCENCE

MY JOURNEY THROUGH POEMS

SMITHA SATYEN

I would like to dedicate this book to my dad,. It was he who induced into me the love for reading and made me a logophile. Thanks dad. Wherever you are, hope I made you proud.

Contents

Contents

Preface

This book 'REMINISCENCE' is very special for me. This being my second anthology of poems to be published. Each poem is a journey through my meory some I imagined, some I witnessed, some my musings while confronting life's situations, while some I have literally lived . Through this book of mine, I invite the readers into the humble abode of my soul and witness it with an open mind. Thank you.

1. BEING A POET.....

My quill has the will
To change this world
But only if you let me
Scribble my thoughts
On the parchment paper
When inspiration surge
Words stumble over one another
Waiting to pour out
The pressure cooker whistles for attention
Saying the daal is cooked
When I sit lost in facination
Enjoying the beauty of the rising sun
Verses begin to flow fluently
Waiting for me to pen
A yell echoes," Chai lao"
Excited to the toes Iam sometimes
To write something really worthwhile
Each line meticulously planned
Forceful enough to bring about a revolution
But I have breakfast to serve my hungry battalion
Amidst the never-ending beck and call
Finishing chores attending phone
Clearing doubts of my pestering tots

Resolving prudently their never ending brawls
Many of my compositions crashed, before take off
Yet I do try my level best
Making muse of my domestic humdrum
Using few as inspiration, ignoring some
Stealing precious moments to compose
For being called poet is really worth all the chaos..

3. CHILDHOOD BLISS

Life has become so stressful
Stuck in the maze of keep pace
With the chaotic mayhem around us
We often forget how to really love
All-around seeing only impending doom
Anxieties and worries follow us
Like a loyal shadow in the sun
Getting larger and larger
The more on it we focus
Leaving us under cloud of gloom
Here's a simple placebo for start
Take some soap and water drops
Lather it in your hands
Make an 'O' with your thumb & digit
& Blow your worries into the froth
Let the bubbles soar gently up
Like magical rainbow hued orbs
Floating & dancing with the wind
Watch as it goes higher & higher
And burst away with a pop
Soon you are having fun
Being like a child again
All your anxieties just vanish

Dispersed into thin air
While you heave a sigh of relief
So mesmerized are you by the game
Forgotten are your grown-up ways
You laugh and skip in pure glee
Unperturbed about what others say
Engrossed in the moment of blissfulness
Remember how it was years back
How strangers easily became chums
Just with a smile that instantly connects
Race, caste, colour, status never did matter
You mix up as easily as sugar in water
What did change as we grow up
Is it the education that altered us?
Losing sight of all the magic
Dissecting it with tools of logic
Squeezing away fun out of every thing
Let out the child hidden within you
Let it show you how life is to be lived
Nothing is worth losing your peace
Do everything that puts smile on your face
Setting an example for world to chase...

4. THE CAFE ACROSS THE STREET

Painted graffiti walls,
Radiating cheerfulness
Aroma of coffee,
So varied in flavors
With mouth watering cookies,
And tantalizing brownies
Invariably you end up
Licking your fingers clean
A mad mix of tables
of every size and shape
Accompanied by chairs and stools
Cramped up in the delightful space
Noise of laughter and shrieks
Sometimes hushed conversation speaks
Still prominently in the background
Soulful jazz music rings
My favorite place since my school days
That's the Decafe cafe',
Just across the street
Chartered to my every emotions
Witnessed as I grew from kid to adolescent
Many a string of boyfriends

And even some lonely sojourn
This place has been my womb
Where I felt most at home
From my chocolate milkshake
to tea black without sugar
From teensy weensy skirts
Or to tailored formals
This place had embraced
my every weird fashion sense
From my very first kiss to
Weeping over many a heart break
Celebrating my graduation
To mourning over losing my pageant
Fond memories reverberate within these walls
Soothing my frayed nerves
When I loose my marbles
The small twin seater table in red
Set in the far corner near a large lancet
Overlooking the busy noisy street
Has been known to be mine
Unconsciously reserved for me
From mugging up my notes
To cramming for my dreaded boards
Scribbling my silly verses
That now I have lost count of
To my first novela which is in progress
This Cafe across the street

Is the home away from home....

5. YOU & ME

Similar like twins
Yet contrary like chalk and cheese
While I'm demure and shy
You are a whirlwind
I chose to be soft spoken
You push forth with arrogance
When I seek to be invisible
You stand out like a sore thumb
Screaming for attention
Iam insecure in my own skin
Low in confidence I sink.
You soar in the skies free
Not least bothered of the world
Dancing your way to success
Achieving all that you desire
You are none other than me
As I see in my dreams
What I strive to desperately be
But am locked in the prison
Of my own making.

6. DEPRIVED JOY

Standing on the corner of the street
Scared and hungry and cold was he
Sparkle in his eyes was dimmed
Lips turned downwards and grim
Shirt in tatters hung limply
On his bony shoulders blades
Too big was his pants
held to his waist by a dirty twine
Twig like thin legs protruding from beneath
Caked with dust and blemishes few
He shivered slightly in the evening breeze
Trying to be brave for himself
Beg he did not want to
But mouths he needed to feed
Work he was ready to do
But none would hire him
Child employment was a crime
But letting someone go hungry
Was it not an unredeemable sin?
The streetlight above him
Shone upon him an eerie glow
Deepening the shadows under his eyes
Yet bathing him in yellowish halo

None gave him a second glance
Maybe trying to strangle their own conscience
When our own child makes a slight whimper
We are all so in attention
This child too deserves the love
Can't we spare him some..?
Take a moment to wipe his tear
Dress him up in clothes neat
Feed him with a smile
And watch his eyes sparkle
The joy you feel in your heart
Is, believe me indescribable
Every child has the right
To enjoy its childhood
Every child's mind is like a fertile land
If you sow on it beautiful seeds
Of kindness and love infinite
It's future will be fragrant
Carrying the act all through his life
Or when he grows to be a thorny plant
Don't you think we as the society too
Need to partake the blame...??

7. .... AND THEN I PENNED IT DOWN

Introvert that I'm
Meeting strangers freaks me out
No knowing what to do
To be honest or mask my feelings true
I just absorb all I see
....and then I pen it down
26 alphabet in my platoon
Changing forever their alignment
To suit my varied emotions
Until I feel that euphoric moment
I can't anymore resist the temptation
....and then I pen it down.
When life feels low
The push seems to just go
All you can do is just wonder
Giving up all hope, just surrender
I just wipe away that ugly frown
.......and then I pen it down
Sometimes when I'm excessively happy
Without any rhyme or reason to explain it
A huge smile on my lips
Eyes twinkling merrily

I adorn my joy as my sparkling crown
....and then I pen it down
At the break of dawn or twilight
When the sky is at its vibrant best
I soak in its blissfull essence
Eternally grateful for all that I can feel
Thoughts that makes me unique
....and then I pen it down.
Whatever life has to offer
I accept it with grace
Sometimes stumbling sometimes flying
Weaving it into meaningful phrase
Trying to infuse it into verses
....and then I pen it down
Years pass in a blink of an eye
Looking back at my journey I proudly smile
I do miss being a carefree innocent child
But what I have become is no mean fact
A poem slowly evolves, with myself as my muse
.....and then I pen it down.

8. CHILDHOOD DAYS

Childhood days
Life's best phase
Unfortunately,
We realise too late
When just faded memories remain
Looking back on those blissfull times
Ears still ring with the sounds
Of the bottle cap wind chimes
Made so proudly with our own hands
When sleep was like punishment
Staying home, not short of imprisonment
World outside was so beautiful
Like looking through a kaleidoscope
Chasing butterflies, rolling on grass
Jumping in puddles, dancing in rain
Floating paper boats in streams
Flying kites , or climbing trees
Streaking barefoot through the lanes
Ready to face the moms wrath when time came
Fights and squabbles among siblings and friends were Frequent
But grudges were rare and easily forgotten
A few sweetmeats were enough

To shift the mode from war to peace
Discrimination racism were words foreign
Friends were either smiling snow flake
Or sweet chocolate
Just being among friends
Were reasons of pleasures infinite
Speaking one's mind was a virtue
Dreams always seemed to be true
Tears were easy , unabashed and momentary
Smiles bright, innocent pure and genuine
Eyes still believed in magic
Without the boring reasoning of logic
Still we delved, in the false illusion
That growing up was all fun.
Wish we could rewind time
And be the carefree, naughty
Innocent, child once again....

9. THE TUMBLING MEMORY

When I was a child
I was just a little kid
All the grown ups around me
To me seemed like colossus
I used to look up in wonder
Longing to be big myself
Now I regret those whimpy wishes
And yearn to be little again
Those carefree childhood days
When life seemed so easy
Laughing aloud, crying louder
No time to sit and contemplate
Every thing was magic, around us
Until logic raised it's ugly head
One such memory still clings
Always making me smile
How I came out unscathed and alive
Is still a mystery unsolved
Merely a tot all of four
Following her sibling blindly around
Copiying everything he did
Was all I ever wanted to accomplish.

On a beautiful summer evening
Visiting an old acquaintance's abode
My brother and his friend
Set forth on an expedition of sorts
Climbing a hillock in front of his house
And seeing the elders busy in chitchat
I too tagged along
To my tiny eyes it was no less then a mountain
Walking carefully the way they lead
Putting one foot ahead of another,
Not looking much afar
Soon we reached the summit
Where stood a dilapidated Ganesh temple
The view I must say was just spellbinding
Houses looked so tiny
People like ants scurrying around
And the sun sinking behind the horizon
The scenario was just mesmerizing
Soon the daylight began to ebb
It was time to get back
The task seemed more daunting than I thought
Not waiting for them to guide the way
Neither thinking of what the consequences be
I took the easiest way I could think of
Recklessness being a habit
Without looking right or left, I leaped
Unable to maintain the momentum

Inertia doing its job
I just bounced a few times
Like an Indian rubber ball
Then rolled down the to the flat ground
not unlike a pile of dough
Luckily for me I just ended up
With just a few painful shiners
Badly shaken nerves,
And nursing a hugely bruised ego
To narrate the story of my adventure
Right to this day my brother and his friend
Tease me rotten for my stupidity
But Iam happy it happened
Holding dear the memory
Of the naughty reckless me..

10. I WISH I COULD.....

I Wish I Could......

I wish I could......
Sit and gaze at the sunrise
Let its beauty mesmerize
But that's just not happening
For mouths hungry wait to be fed
I wish I could......
Watch the roses bloom
Kissed by the drops of dew
But such lazy minutes for me are few
For Iam the maid the cook the cleaning crew
I wish I could .....
Enjoy sipping my coffee hot
Sitting on the window lost in thought
But then my kids scream for attention
For one has lost his sock
I wish I could.....
Just find time to pen a verse
Put my myriad imagination into words
But that's a luxury too much to ask
For the cooker whistle pierces my seance
I wish I could ....
Just be invisible

To see what difference it would make
May be they will miss me for a day or two
Then everything will be normal again
I wish I could.....
Just bottle up my feelings
And these emotions turbulent
Seal it and fling it into some ocean
For leading a life catering to my whims
does sometimes irks my conscience...

11. I OFTEN WONDER....

I often wonder...
Why this life sucks
Stealing all my pleasures
What have I ever done
To deserve this curse
I often wonder ....
After a night so soothing
Where my dreams comfort me
Why this day dawns
Blinding me with its realities
I often wonder...
When the whole world rejoices
Celebrating moments of happiness
Why is mine always snatched away
When it reaches my finger tips
I often wonder...
The face that stares from my mirror
Does it even know what's in store for her
Floating merrily on the bubble of joy
Soon will burst, crashing her fragile hopes
I often wonder.......
What it feels to be

When little joys cling to me
Soaking me with its fragrance
Leaving no place for regrets
I often wonder......
What it would be like
To go away somewhere
Into some lonely abandoned island
With just me and my precious nature
No body to judge me for my ways
No body to make me dance to their wills
No body to dictate my priorities
No body to point out and mock my mistakes
Just me seeking joy of living
Writing to appease my very soul
With no nagging thoughts of tomorrow's...

12. MY QUEST FOR HAPPINESS

According to science
It's the chemical that shines
When serotonin, dopamine, oxytocin
Runs around in your blood stream
Causing your spirits to lift
And eyes to sparkle with mirth
So it's all from within
But needs external influence
To trigger off the reaction
When I was a kid , tiny
With vocabulary few , not many
Mamma's smile and touch was enough
To make me giggle happily
Then sweets began to tempt me
And happiness was sucking on a candy
Slowly the horizons opeaned
Happiness took many a disguises
Going to school was all about
Meeting friends , sharing tiffin boxes
What we learned was soon forgotten
But the knowedge did enrich us
For a successful career we were besotten

As I grew into a teen
Eyes of my crush I sought often
Making my heart flutter,
Dreaming all sorts of fantasies
But amidst family and friends
Happiness was at its highest
Earning my first pay cheque
Seeing pride of my parents
The admiration in my siblings eyes
When I brought gifts for them
Slowly added to my store of happy moments
As I grew older, maturity invariably dawned
Priorities changed
What once seemed so precious
Started loosing it's appeal
Chasing targets, meeting deadlines
Closing projects presentation and deals
Few moments of respite was big relief
Amidst those too were special moments
Getting married ,tying a knot for life
Withing a few moments a stranger
Becomes the centre of your universe
All your world now revolves around him
You seek your happiness and joy
In his smiles, and naughty glances
When together like a miracle
You create another life

Without seeing, just knowing.
A seed growing within your womb
That's the moment of pure bliss.
Holding my children for the first time
Caring for them, watching them grow
Their first smile, first word,
first stumbling step , all left it's mark
On my happiness chart.
Now during a lonely night
Lying on a hammock staring the starry sky
My life reels before my eyes like a cinemascope
With the gentle breeze soothing my skin
Clouds gliding past revealing the moon
I sigh aloud , this too is happiness
Soul is at peace ,
so detached from the chaos of the world
And Iam just happy for no reason
Isn't that the best kind of happiness...!!!

13. QUARANTINE

Isolation....
It seems the world has cut me off
As if the mere sight of me repulse
Ones whom I thought loved my company
Now seems to be entirely lost
Has the illness messed up my brain cells
That now being with me bores them to death
Stuck in the prison of four walls
Just a barred window to gaze out
With my ever faithful mogra plant
Sitting quietly on the ledge , blooming
I talk to it all my woes and feelings
It nods at me being all understanding
Never an opinion it has to offer
Still connects with me at a level far deeper
It feels bad to be a burden on all
Unable to do even a little to help
How long can I stare into this rectangle
A poor substitute it is for human touch
Though it's my only link with world
But I feel I'm in a different universe
I so miss my normalcy
But hate to spread the epidemic gastly

How I wish I could rewind time
To those days not too far behind
Sharing anecdotes and facts rare and true
Discussion with fervor world affairs
Now all seems so monotonous
Nor are my writings hitting the mark
All the strings that linked me with others
I grapple at it with all my might to save
Agry, upset and cranky I have become
Tears threatening to spill every instant
I know I have to see this through
Giving up for me is not an excuse
Control my emotions before it wrecks
Alienates every relationship through words harsh
I know very well this time too will pass
But getting through each moment , seems impossible.

14. BEING A MOTHER

The moment you know
Everything sort of changes
A tiny life pulsating within you
Is no less than natures miracle
Your whole perspective changes,
So does your priorities
Your whole life now revolves
Around this tiny entity
Unseen, unheard
Yet you're fiercely protective
The love that you feel is
Totally indescribable
Reading books, scrolling the internet
You leave no stone unturned
To find what for him is best
Trying to be calm,
when all you feel is anxiety
Calling up your doctor
Doubting as if deliberately
The slim figure that you maintained religiously
Which you once carried with pride
Often an envy of your dearest friends
Now begin filling up in most unlikely places

Making you look like a sack more than anything else
Yet you look at the mirror blushing
Gently touching the tummy,
where the angel is resting
Morning nausea, giddiness and sickness
Yet your spirits always soaring
When you see your angel ,its first glimpse
On the monitor of the USG
Your eyes anxious, it looks so adorable
Waving arms and legs
As the time of delivery nears
Swelling at the ankles, blotchy is your face
When you walk it looks a duck waddling,
Yet the eternal glow on your face is mind blowing
Then the moment arrives
exonerating pain starts increasing by the minute
Decreasing is the gap between....the pain goes on and on
Now unable to stop yelling
Terrible thoughts bombard my mind
I shall go through hell I pray
But let my little one must come to no harm
In the hospital, nurses hover around
Paying no attention
as I try to quell my cries
When it becomes unbearable I trash
The nurses shift me to the delivery bed
So cruelly indifferent they seem

Thousands of cases every day the see
Nothing exciting for them, it seems
After like ages and many a terrifying moments
A final contraction that shook my soul
My baby was out in the world
All pink and soft it looked
So fragile and tender
The doctor severed the final bond
That till now held us together .
For the first time I held him.
I couldn't stop the tears from flowing
So overwhelming was that moments feeling
Just closed my eyes ,thanking God
For the blessing, I now held in my arms
I touched his soft pink palm
His minute fingers clutched it tight
As I fed him for the first time
An inexplicable feeling of delight
Every thing was so special about him
Even in his sleep I just keep looking
His large eyes when he stared at me
Its puckering pink lips that yawned
His tiny wail of cry even that was music
Nothing about my boy was ordinary to me
He was my brightest star...
When I brought it home
I needed everything sterile

Looked at everything with a critical eye
People started commenting, I had OCD
A timer forever by my side
My doctor chastened me....loosen up a bit
My son grew like a weed,,
he had a healthy appetite
But I thought he ate too little
Most horrifying days were his vaccinations
How could I let someone poke a painful needle
Even though it was for his protection
We both invariably cried on those days
He began to crawl got under everyone's feet
Had to keep doors locked least he crawl outside
Slowly he started taking unsteady steps
Seeing that I was the proudest
Calling me mama for the first time
I could feel my heart burst with joy
How fast the years passed I couldn't gauge
My world was totally limited to this tiny tot
His first day of school I vividly remember
Smartly dressed in uniform, looked all grown up
Holding my hand tight, me too hung on to him
First time in life I'm gonna be away from him
When he let go my hand eyes brimming
Lips trembling, looking back at every step
I too couldn't hold back my tears
Waiting outside the school for the neverending 3 hours

Anxious, nervous, fearful, will everything be ok?
When the bell rang the children poured out
He walked out holding hand with another smart tot
I realised, my son has grown up,
Made his first friend in world
Years went by as if in a haze
As he grew up, I too grew with him
Our interests changed
Fights, tantrums, quarrels
many a light moments
His birthdays , birth of his baby sister
(Shall tell about it another day)
Now he is a handsome guy of 23
When with me still a kid in shorts
When outside he is responsible and smart
But with me still behaves like a 4yr old tot

15. THE DEW DROP

Tiny little drop of water
Settled on the blade of grass
Wobbling a little in the wind
Yet it held on for life
Shivering with the leaf in cold
Waiting patiently for the dawn
Suddenly a glow appeared
On the eastern horizon
Lighting up the skies in hues
Of breathtaking purples & pinks
The dew looked on awe
Hypnotized by the splendour
She waited with bated breath
For the majestic sun to rise
Riding on his golden chariot
Up into the vast skies
Kiss her with his rays of light
And redeem her ephemeral life
Slowly the clouds parted
Singed in flames by the sun's ire
Making way for it to proceed
Relieve the world of grim darkness
Smiling down he spotted the tiny dew

With its rays a kiss he blew
With the kiss of light the dew blushed
Glowing radiantly like a newly wed
Sparkling like a diamond on its perch
Like a studded crown on nature's head
Slowly with the breeze it withered
Done with its soft sweet dewy tenure
Look at it carefully for once
I know you too will be spell bound
This tiny drop in this vast universe
Encompassing within it a watery world
Swirling with colours of rainbow
Shining with its eternal glow
Forget everything you surely will
Enchanted by this beautiful dewy morning

16. MY CAMERA AND ME

Wish I could capture all that I can see
The views which tickles the shutterbug in me
To freeze those beautiful moments
And share it with the world gleefully
I wait eagerly every morn to catch
The rising sun behind the coconut palms
Peeping through it's long leaves
Like looking out of window grills
Dew drops glistening on the grass blades
As if studded with diamonds rare
When the sun kisses it with love
Watch it blush in colours of rainbow
When raindrops slide over the window panes
Leaving a trail of murk and grime
As it swirls merrily in the puddle it makes
That's beauty indeed with a different take .
The tiny lavender blooms amidst the weeds
Beauty and grace subtle, albeit from view hid
They too exude their own uncanny charm
You just need to know where to look.
The smiling faces of a kids at play
Eyes laughing with naughty mischief

A smile fleeting, here now gone now,
You wish you could just hold time still
Wrinkled cheeks of old granny
Eyes now dull but filled with wisdom deep
Looking into space glowing with unshed tears
Remembering the trauma of bygone years
Ever watched a cow with its young calf
Adoringly looking at it with gentle eyes
Or the dog admonishing it's pups
When they stray away from its watchful eyes
A vibrant kingfisher patiently waiting
For a juicy morsel to prey
An eagle gliding high in the sky
combing the grounds with his keen sight
A tiny rose bud shrouded in green
Slowly shyly revealing a little daily
Until finally it attains it's full bloom
At each stage enthralling; a boon
The sprightly butterfly with its radiant wings
Fluttering around seeking nectar from flower's womb
The bees buzzing about without a care
Making sweet honey to fill their combs
A naughty squirrel scampering about
Hiding nuts in tree holes and grass
Keeping a wayward eyes on the human lot
They too know our unscrupulous ways
When the sun sinks into the horizon

Painting the sky in a deluge of vibrant hues
That keeps changing every second
Leaving one stunned beyond words
When the sky adorns it's cruelean cloak
Stars in millions slip out to shine
And majestically the moon makes its way
Bathing the world in it's silvery maze.
So much beauty all around me
Describing it justly my vocabulary's scarce
I wish I could capture through my camera lens
To relieve those moments when blues hits me thence.

17. THE HOME COMING

There it stands lonely dilapidated
Dark against the dawn painted sky
Overgrown with creepers wild
Like some mansion haunted by sprites
The iron gate now squeaked in protest
From years of lying neglected
The path that once shone bright
Now barely visible under the grass knee high
Bushing roughly against the legs
As if in awe of sensing human again
After a decade of being ignored
Not a soul had ever turned to tend
The pond that once rippled with life
Is deathly still as if frozen in time
The once transparent sparkling cool waters
Stands covered with green fungi
Suffocating the water lying dead within
Even the steps leading are blanketed in moss green
The sida shrubs that nurtured my dark tresses
That mom painstakingly collected and crushed
Murmuring endearments, cajoling me patiently
Agaist my childish tantrums , getting me to sit still

Now they too are lost like those nostalgic moments
Obscured by weeds of mundane memories
The mango saplings that I once planted
Waiting and watching daily for it to sprout
Now stands tall against the skies
It's foliage spreading like a crocheted umbrella vast
Causing light and shadows to dance merrily
Laden with fruits temptingly juicy
The cowshed once my grandpa's pride
That he built with his own hands
Where white and brown cows once stood
Happily munching the golden hay and green grass
Mooing to grab ones attention
Now looks forlorn & so bored with life
An eerie creek renders the pregnant silence
Making a chill run down the spine
As the thick wooden doors open
The cacophony of flapping wings echoes
Startled avians flustered, take flight
From the their long ago adopted abode
Dust swirling as if dancing a tango
In the golden beam of light that slithers in
Through the gap in the window shutters
I feel as I have been transported back
Like some magic portkey at work
Iam the happy naughty cheerful child again
Memories suddenly springs to life

As if an animated scene unfolds
On a pop up greeting card
The old wreck of an house
Once again throbbing with happy spirit
Each corner spic and span yet lived in
Pattering of feet running up &down the stairs
Sound of laughter or of mom's melodious songs
Aroma of delicacies wafting from the kitchen
Makes my mouth salivate and stomach growl
Tongue turning nostalgic with the taste remembered
How I desperately wish I could turn back the clock
I go from one dust filled room to another
Every paint peeling corner bursting with cache
Some sweet some bitter, some downright hilarious
But stirring a sensitive chord deep within the heart
The warmth I felt here in the cold empty dilapidated house
Was for my wandering restless soul, a homecoming.

18. THE BARBER'S CHAIR

Holding my Pa's finger
As if it was my life line
Slowly I walked along the street
Awed by the wonders all around
The world seemed so big
To my tiny eyes
We stopped outside a dianty shop
Where all the strangers smiled seeing pa
Inside a burly man shouted
I hid behind pa's legs. feeling scared
His bald head and bushy whiskers
Menacing it looked, shivering when he laughed
Pa lifted me in his arms
Took me inside, I clung to him
Soothing me he made me sit
On a blue chair with soft cushions
It swallowed me up almost whole
Both of them laughed as if a big joke
They put a plank across its arm rest
Making me sit upon that
I shivered and gulped ,
Trying hard to be brave

He came towards me with scissors & comb
I really thought it was my end
After the ordeal was finally over
Still sniffling catching my breath
Leaving my crowning glory behind
As bald as him now I too am
I looked at the chair with fury
It was the monster of my nightmare
It was just the first of many to come
Me and that chair were meant to meet again
Many a times with my dear pa
Then it was on my own
It was not just a barbers shop
But a portal into information world
Lot of topics were volleyed over
World issues to gossips local
Political debate over tea and samosas
Laughing over the satirical state of middle class
Rejoicing over every little pleasure
Condolences offered genuine to those crossed over
On the blue chair I sat absorbing all
From childhood to teen to adolescent
Buba, as I called him, was my coiffeur
From advices about my mane care
To giving tips to cruise through life
Sometimes I did his interference resent
Yet I grudgingly applauded his wisdom

Sitting on the wobbly blue chair
As I aged so did Buba & the blue chair
He presided over the assembly daily
Regaly on his throne now much repaired
While his heirs took over the pruning
I too left to seek my reckoning
Taking along many treasures in my memory
Nowhere ever did I find those blissful charade
I flew back hopping countries
To perform the last rites of my pa
He left us all in his sleep smiling
Missing him with regrets many
Wishing desperately to turn time back
Heavy hearted and eyes brimming
Buba stood by me stoically
Pulling me into the blue chair once again
Words were not required, neither did he utter any
Slightly his hands tremored as he shaved my head
We both missed the one person we loved
The void that no one ever could fill
Now with my own progeny away exploring
Back I'm in the place where I began
I traversed the street walking stick in hand
Head totally bald except for a few stubborn strands
I stood before a sparkling new saloon
Where once stood Buba's empire
Inside I went more out of curiosity

Nobody as much spared me a glance
Some one came and hugged me tight
It was Buba's son, Adil, my old friend
He took me inside where he now alone resides
There in a corner still stood the blue chair

19. THE IVORY TOWER

Amidst the chaos
In a world of my own
Immune to the cacophony
My mind is at peace
Is it love or insanity
Society gossip, calling me names
Some sympathize ,some act wary
As if I'm afflicted by a virus deadly
Not following them blindly
But happy in my weirdness
They try to evoke in me emotions
Some thing that connects me to them
Trying every trick old and new
Praising, bulliying, insulting , even some sarcasm
I just smile and watch them fume
I know not what they expect,
I know not why they pester,
Trying to fit me in their mould,
Yet expecting me to be conspicuous,
Until I deliberately shut them all out.
I do what I feel right,
Happy in my own plight,

Enjoying every bit of life,
Even through tears, smiling,
And they think I've lost my marbles.
In this world of man eat man
Every soul engaged in a race against time
Running in circles over and over
Scared of tomorrow they mentally cower
I'm madly happy in My Ivory Tower

20. NEW BEGININGS

No matter what transpired
Let go of what expired
Mulling over it won't change
Nor do you own a time machine
So just close the door to past
And make a new beginning
Worrying won't get you far
Rather distract you that's for sure
Failures many you may face
Leave on you it's scar as trace
Disecting it just postpones healing
Get a closure, make a new beginning
Life has its ways of teaching
Every setback isn't a curse
It could be in disguise a blessing
A Kick , a punch a knock a shove
Hurt it may, but absolutely necessary
For you to make a new beginning
Sunsets may be spectacular
Night calm serene and restful
It's also a ruse to get you thinking
Of what was and how for you it's been
Go over the lessons you learned

Offer prayer of gratitude for everything.
When the dawn breaks over the horizon
Painting the skies in hues mesmerizing
Birds chirping their cacophony merrily
The whole nature bursting with spontanity
Wake up with a new hope sparkling
It's a new day, a new life, a new beginning.

21. HORIZON

Horizon
Is it a myth or an illusion
The place where sky humbly bows
To kiss the earth in adoration
Isn't it a magical landmark
That gobbles up the sun
As the earth turns dark
Only to spit it out at break of dawn
As epitome of hope it is seen
A land where no one's been
Still urges you to keep going
Luring you with a view spellbinding
It is how you perceive
It's all about perspective
Either limit to your imagination
Or gateway to your dreams

22. DOING NOTHING

Why be engaged all the while
Doing something or the other
Scrolling on the mobile phone
Slowly stiff is your neck and shoulder
Thinking of past or future
Until deep frown lines appear
Planning in advance for years ahead
When tomorrow is all but uncertain
Let go of everything for a little while
Unburden your shoulder of the heavy pile
Go outside and enjoy some sunshine
Amidst the beautiful nature divine
Breathe in the fresh fragrant air
Ticklish you feel as it plays with your hair
Listen to the sounds around you
Chirping birds, rustling leaves , gurgling brook
Suddenly an aeroplane zooms by over head
Make you want to jump and wave
oblivious of all the perplexed stares
Feeling like your childhood is here to stay
Watch the blooming flowers sway
As if making funny gestures at you
making you invariably smile wide

throwing caution in the air.
Squint your eyes towards the sky blue
Cloudless, like a canvas ready for use
Waiting for you to paint your imaginations
In vibrant hues that you lovingly choose
You never know how easily time slips
In every moment feel the pure bliss
Weaving beautiful memories worth treasuring
While you are busy, happily doing nothing.

23. RIPPLES OF TIME

Sitting in my lonely sojourn
Lost in myriad musings of my own
Barely feeling the wind that caress
Playing merrily with my tresses
Unaware of the world around.
My swaying feet skim over water
Causing ripples chase eachother
Edges of my lips lift in a smile
Is it some wayward memory
or the kick of red wine
Chirping bird's soothing harmony
Enchanting nature's delightful symphony
Embracing me in comforting company
Healing slowly my heart's agony
calmimg me in my melancholy
Listlessly I tear each page
from the journals of my past age
Some worded with tears of pain
some decorated with love serene
Watch it drift away gently downstream

24. EMOTIONS

Random deep and confusing
Sometimes happy sometimes distressing
They just surge within you, unannounced
How shall I deal with I've no clue
I wish I knew how to react
When out of the blue sadness strikes
Lips tremble , heart feel heavy & tight
All I want is hide somewhere and cry
When the sky is cloudy , dark and angry
Everything around seems so gloomy
Inside my heart begins to dread
I know its a forcast for something really bad
No matter how hard I try
I still keep missing the mark
I know not where am I going wrong
Frustrated against this life, being so unfair
When he looks into my eyes
Holds my hand and whispers his love
Thousands of butterflies flutters within me
I become speechless , yet my smile says it all
When my baby looks up and smiles
Gaping at me with her innocent eyes
I just feel my heart melt inside

Indescribable is that feeling of joy
All I can do is take a pen and scribble
Try to portray them in words feeble
But scarcely could I justify the feeling
For emotions,needs to be felt
just can't be explained

24. A RENDEZVOUS WITH MYSELF

At the hour of twilight
When the sun bids adieu
The sky bestowing it's reverence
Painting the clouds in plethora of hues
I sat stunned, watching the magic unfold.
Lost in the alluring milieu
The world faded away from view
Left in the entire universe
Was my soul, spirit...just me
Totally and entirely at bliss
In the serene comforting solitude
I heard a tiny whispering sound
Biwildered I looked around
But no one was to be found
It was my own inner voice profound
Never had I heeded to it
Not knowing ever that it exists
It poured out all its greviences
Mainly for my utter ignorance
Believing entirely on the world's opinion
A long conversation we had
Looking me in the eye it did stare

Opening before me my hidden scars
Letting it bleed it's venom all
That had been eroding my sanity for long
Always trying I was to please others
Paying little attention to my own pleasures
Searching for acceptance around
Often ending up dejected, spirits low
When all I needed my soul within it held
When I woke from my reverie
The night was already quite young
The crescent moon floated high
Peeping through the fluffy clouds
Across the star studded prussian blue sky
Everything was crystal clear,
Like awakening from a turbulent nightmare
Wisdom dawned, never too late to accept
That rendezvous with myself, changed my mindset
Self love is indeed the essence of being best..

25. MY TRIBUTE TO DAD

Dad , papa, father
What can I say
Falling short of words
For nothing I write for you
Can ever justify your worth
I was your favourite
You tolerated all my whims
Stood by me guiding me
Letting me explore my skills
With words of wisdom ready
You passed on to me your passion
Reading, solving crosswords, enjoying outdoors
I try my level best, papa
To follow in your steps of humbleness
And of living within ones means
You were a man of few words
Yet your actions spoke quite aloud
Your life is truly an example
An inspiration to a dignified existence
We had our arguments and sparks
But it only had brought us more close
I never in my widest dreams considered

That one day you'll leave my side
That too was so sudden, I yet can't grasp
Wish I had you for some more years
Listening to your experiences
Partake a little more of your vast wisdom
Telling you all my dreams
How I wish you were with me now
Watch how your tiny angel had grown
From a shy little girl to a confident lady
Facing the world with spine of steel
Watch your eyes shine with pride
Seeing what all your princess has achieved
And how the little kid you held in your arms
Has now grown into a handsome young man
Though my kids have never seen you
They know you as their hero Gramps
Coz' I never can stop regaling them with stories
Of my childhood with you beside me
Wherever you are, I hope you're happy
Living a life you loved to lead
We do really miss your presence terribly
Ever day every hour every minute
I may never have said it to you aloud
But I guess you knew it all along
You were always my super hero dad
And my love for you shall never fade...
Love you lots Papa...

Printed by Libri Plureos GmbH in Hamburg, Germany